THE UNLEARNED LESSON

The Role of Alcohol and Drug Misuse in Homicides Perpetrated by People with Mental Health Problems

A Study of Seventeen Reports of Inquiries into Homicides by Mentally Ill People

by Mike Ward & Claire Applin

With a foreword by Eric Appleby (Director, Alcohol Concern) & Roger Howard (Director, Standing Conference on Drug Abuse)

Supported by
Alcohol Concern &
Standing Conference on Drug Abuse

Wynne Howard Books
1998

Dedicated to our parents
Mavis & John Ward
Kathleen & Donald Compton

Published by
Wynne Howard Publishing
London
CR8 5ET
Great Britain
0181-763-8944

First Published February 1998

British Library Cataloguing in Publication Data. A catalogue record card for this book is available from the British Library.

ISBN 0 9525571 4 2

FOREWORD

Eric Appleby - Alcohol Concern
& Roger Howard - Standing Conference on Drug Abuse

Each homicide inquiry report represents a particular tragedy. The despair of the victim's family and friends, the trauma of those who have attempted to care for the killer and the suffering of the killer are displayed for all to see. They do not make easy reading under any circumstances. Nonetheless they have proved invaluable in focusing attention on the causes of homicides by people with mental health problems.

We are aware that some people now argue that the inquiry process has gone too far. The messages from each report say many of the same things. Themes such as lack of communication, need for better risk assessment, and greater continuity of care in the community are emerging from report after report. The time has come, it is argued, to act on the conclusions rather than continue to search for problems.

This report argues, however, that one very important lesson has not been learnt - the role of substance misuse. Drug and alcohol misuse clearly is a major feature of many of the homicides covered by the inquiries. In some cases it appears to be a major contributory factor in the killing itself, in other cases it is part of the background complex web of problems which led to the homicide. In some cases it is even parental alcohol misuse which has been a contributory factor.

That alcohol and drug misuse should feature in the reports is not a surprise. Both Alcohol Concern and the Standing Conference on Drug Abuse have long recognised that people who misuse substances and people who have mental health problems are not always two separate groups. Evidence from both the UK and abroad has highlighted that many people with mental health problems also misuse drugs or alcohol and that conversely a worrying number of substance misusers, especially problematic misusers, experience mental health problems of many and varied kinds. It is inevitable that alcohol and drug misuse should be a factor in the reports.

The level of involvement of drug and alcohol misuse in the inquiries is much more surprising. Only one report of those studied makes no mention of any misuse of substances and in a majority of reports such misuse is a significant feature of the case. This statistic ought not to surprise us, as some kinds of drug misuse and, in particular, alcohol misuse are strongly associated with violent crime. However, as both our organisations have argued it is symptomatic of the "cinderella" status of substance misuse services that the mental illness is the overwhelming preoccupation but that the drug and alcohol misuse are underplayed. This imbalance helps no-one, not the victims nor the perpetrators, not alcohol or drug misuse services nor even mental health services.

By emphasising simply the role of mental ill health we are in danger of continuing erroneously to stigmatise some people with mental health problems as "dangerous". Moreover, and from our point of view very importantly, it plays down the vital role that alcohol and drug misuse services must have in the development of effective care in the community.

Above all, however, we must prioritise public safety. The failure to recognise the role of drug and alcohol misuse in homicides means that efforts to prevent future tragedies are being hampered. This important report emphasises the urgent need to develop more comprehensive treatment services for all those who misuse alcohol or drugs.

EXECUTIVE SUMMARY

This study considers the role of alcohol and drug misuse in inquiries into homicides by mentally ill people. External evidence suggests that significant numbers of those people with mental health problems who commit homicides should have a concomitant alcohol or drug misuse problem. The study examines seventeen separate homicide inquiries from the last four years.

Of those seventeen studies fourteen have a marked alcohol or drug misuse component.
In the majority of reports the killer has an identifiable history of alcohol or drug misuse.
In 53% of cases alcohol or drug misuse could be argued to be a major, if not the major, cause of the homicide.

The study highlights the lack of significant recommendations in the inquiries in relation to alcohol or drug misuse.
The study emphasises that this issue needs to be rapidly addressed:

- **to ensure as few people as possible are victims of such killings**
- **to reduce the stigma attached to mental illness because of homicide inquiries**
- **to improve alcohol and drug misuse services**

The study concludes with five recommendations for future action:
1. The Department of Health should immediately initiate further urgent work to research and explore in greater depth the contribution of alcohol and drug misuse to investigated homicides by people with mental health problems.

2. The terms of reference for inquiries should have regard to the role played by alcohol or drug misuse. For example the Paul Smith Inquiry included in its terms of reference the requirement to explore "the appropriateness of the care plan ....in the context of ...his previous psychiatric history including drug and alcohol abuse.(p.7)" This should be standard in all inquiry reports.

3. When appropriate, inquiry reports should make recommendations specifically about the care of the drug and alcohol misuse component of the case.

4. Alcohol and drug misuse services should be routinely circulated with inquiry reports and should consider the lessons for them in those reports.

5. Mental health and alcohol and drug misuse services at both a national and a local level should collaborate to develop better service responses to the often chaotic, dually diagnosed clients presented in inquiry reports. However, this should not be at the expense of the wider group of people with alcohol and drug problems who are also faced with a shortage of appropriate services.

INTRODUCTION

In May 1994 the NHS Executive published "Guidance on the discharge of mentally disordered people and their continuing care in the community" (HSG(94)27). This stipulated that in cases of homicide by people with mental health problems, it is necessary to hold an inquiry which is independent of the providers involved. Of course, this document did not initiate inquiries. There had been inquiries stretching back over two decades prior to that date. However the guidance has certainly increased the regularity with which they occur.

It was a far more tragic turn of events which really brought the inquiry process to public attention. In December 1992 Christopher Clunis stabbed Jonathan Zito, a complete stranger, to death on Finsbury Park underground station, in an unprovoked attack. Clunis was a diagnosed schizophrenic and had a long history of engagement with mental health services. Following the court case, an inquiry was launched into how this care had failed to the extent that led to the death of an innocent man. The Ritchie Report into the Treatment and Care of Christopher Clunis caught the public attention in a way that previous inquiries had failed to achieve. Its vivid description of the way care broke down for Clunis challenged public, politicians and professionals alike.

Unfortunately, the need for inquiries has not disappeared. Since the Clunis inquiry there have been many further inquiries. Indeed so familiar has the inquiry process become that some are questioning the usefulness of these processes. Even one of the reports (The Grey Report) asks rhetorically "Are lessons being learnt from these reports? Can past mistakes teach us how to deal appropriately with similar future problems? Are the recommendations contained in these reports heeded and acted upon?" (p.5)

This study is not going to enter into that debate. Nor is it the place to record the details of all the reports or to summarise their contents. That task has already been undertaken by The Zito Trust in their excellent publication "Learning The Lessons". For anyone interested in the complete picture, there can be no better publication. It details all the inquiries from the last few years and records the recommendations in a helpful and telling manner.

The purpose of this brief pamphlet is much more limited. It is to highlight the ignored thread which runs through many of these reports - alcohol and drug misuse.

THE ROLE OF ALCOHOL AND DRUG MISUSE IN HOMICIDE INQUIRIES

It is ironic from this point of view that the best known of the reports - Clunis - identifies that alcohol and drug misuse was not a significant issue. This may well have had the unintended effect of concealing that many of the reports reveal the use of drugs or alcohol to be significant contributors to the homicide.

Take for example, the case of Raymond Sinclair who killed his mother in 1994. This homicide was perpetrated while Sinclair was under the influence of alcohol brought to stave off the shakes from alcohol withdrawals he had experienced on waking. As another example one could quote the Newby Report which acknowledges that substance misuse may have been the main cause of the death of hostel worker Jonathan Newby.

Alcohol and drugs are a feature of homicide inquiries. The purpose of this report is to reveal both the extent of that involvement and the degree to which report recommendations have ignored the issue.

That alcohol and illegal drugs should be a factor in these homicides is not surprising. Anyone approaching this topic in complete ignorance of the content of the inquiries, but with a decent knowledge of mental health and substance misuse should expect a reasonable degree of alcohol and drug misuse to be revealed. External evidence from just four sources would be enough to make this point.

Firstly, it is already well known that alcohol is a contributory factor in almost half of murders in this country and that people with alcohol and/or drug problems are twice as likely as those with schizophrenia to be violent. (The University of Manchester / Department of Health's "Learning Materials on Mental Health - Risk Assessment" e.g. p23).

Secondly, the same source identified alcohol and drugs as being a key factor in making a situation more risky (e.g. p12). It further identifies that non-compliance with psycho-active medication is a risk factor and that alcohol and drug misuse is a key contributor to non-compliance. It is a constant plea of the mental health field that people with mental health problems are no more and possibly less dangerous than the general population. However, once alcohol or drugs become a feature of the presentation, the dangers are multiplied. The risk of violence among people with schizophrenia was only 8% compared with 30% for mentally disordered people who also abused substances. (p.24)

Thirdly, evidence from The Report of the Confidential Inquiry into Homicides and Suicides by Mentally Ill People again confirms a link between homicide and alcohol and drug misuse. The Confidential Inquiry was commissioned in 1992 by the Department of Health following consultation with the Royal College of Psychiatrists. Its remit included, among others, to inquire into the circumstances leading up to and surrounding homicides and suicides by people under the care of, or recently discharged by, the specialist psychiatric services.

The Confidential Inquiry's first report identified that in 18% of the homicides on which they had reports alcohol or other non-prescribed substances had been used immediately prior to the killing. (p.26). The report received 110 separate comments on these homicides from those involved. It identifies that in a small number of cases where compliance with treatment had been a problem this was linked to the concurrent use of illicit drugs (p.29). An appendix to the report (p.82) acknowledges that "Intense emotional arousal in the setting of a disturbed interpersonal relationship, sometimes accompanied by disinhibition with alcohol or drugs, is a common feature of many homicides." However, even though substance misuse is identified as a factor in almost one in five homicides, no recommendations are made about tackling this aspect of homicides by people with mental health problems.

Fourthly, evidence from those studying the co-morbidity of mental health and alcohol and drug misuse have long identified the significant overlap between the two diagnoses. For example the book "Dual Diagnosis: Facing The Challenge" by Rorstad and Checinski examines the prevalence of dual diagnosis based on functional psychosis. The prevalence of functional psychosis in the UK population is 4 per 1,000 according to the OPCS. American studies of the severely mentally ill have documented a prevalence of alcohol and drug misuse among this group as high as 50%. Using this figure it can be estimated that in an area of the UK with a population of 500,000, i.e. the size of an average health district, the number of people with functional psychosis and a co-morbid alcohol or drug misuse problem may be in the order of 665. [This calculation is based on the assumption that a population of 500,000 will contain approximately 334,600 in the 16-64 population]

The same book also attempts to make estimates based on figures of the prevalence of alcohol and drug misuse. The OPCS Survey of Psychiatric Morbidity in GB - Bulletin 1 1994 estimates the national prevalence of alcohol dependence to be 4.7% and of drug dependence to be 2.2% in the 16-64 age group. These figures would suggest that within a population of half a million there will be 15,726 alcohol dependent and 7,361 drug dependent individuals. From US studies (e.g. Co-Morbidity of Mental Disorders with Alcohol & Other Drug Abuse - Epidemiologic Catchment Area Study NIMH/ADA 1990) it is known that for people with an alcohol problem, the incidence of a co-morbid mental health problem is likely to be 37% and for those with a drug problem, the incidence will be significantly higher at 53%. This is confirmed by a study at the Maudsley Hospital which suggested that 30-40% of patients with alcohol problems also had an additional diagnosis quoted in Rorstad 1996).

The evidence for the overlap between alcohol and drug misuse and homicide and substance misuse and mental health is overwhelming. **The link between these factors is scarcely surprising. What is surprising is the absence of alcohol and drug misuse from the recommendations of these inquiry reports. "Learning the Lessons" details a long list of over six hundred recommendations and conclusions culled from the inquiries that it reviews. Of these recommendations only four refer to alcohol and drug misuse. A substance misuse specialist can only be startled by the lack of recommendations related to alcohol and drug misuse. It is this imbalance that compels this study.**

METHODOLOGY

This report has looked at seventeen different homicide inquiry reports. These were not randomised to the extent that would satisfy the requirements of a scientific survey. However, the reports listed in this document were simply the first seventeen reports that became available to the authors. Reports with a alcohol and drug misuse element were not sought out, and at least two reports that the authors knew to have an alcohol or drug misuse component were not included because they did not become available. Those reports which became available and were studied but which did not include alcohol and drug misuse elements have been noted as a matter of record.

THANKS
We would like to record our thanks to our valued colleague Joan Rappaport of Surrey Social Services Complex Needs Team for her help with this project. We are also grateful for the support of our colleagues within Surrey Social Services Rita Brewis, Henry Woodall and Liz Parkes. The staff of both Alcohol Concern and the Standing Conference on Drug Abuse have also been very supportive, particularly Sue Baker and Annette Dale-Perrera.

THE REPORTS CONSULTED:

- JONATHAN NEWBY
- THE GREY REPORT
- EB
- MICHAEL BUCHANAN
- BRIAN DOHERTY
- ELLEN AND ALAN BOLLAND
- THE FALLING SHADOW
- RAYMOND SINCLAIR
- JASON MITCHELL
- GILBERT KOPERNIK-STECKEL
- CHRISTOPHER CLUNIS
- PAUL SMITH
- THE WOODLEY TEAM REPORT
- MARTIN MURSELL
- THE VINER REPORT
- OTHER REPORTS CONSULTED

NOTE: The fact that a particular inquiry has been included in this study does not imply that any of the main protagonists were necessarily alcohol or drug misusers. Where this conclusion can be made, it has been highlighted in the text and conclusions of this report and should not be made otherwise.

BIBLIOGRAPHY
The University of Manchester / Department of Health - Learning Materials on Mental Health: Risk Assessment - University of Manchester -1996
Rorstad, Checinski et al - Dual Diagnosis - Facing the Challenge - Wynne Howard Books - 1996
Co-Morbidity of Mental Disorders with Alcohol & Other Drug Abuse - Epidemiologic Catchment Area Study - NIMH/ADA, USA - 1990
Glass 1988
OPCS - Survey of Psychiatric Morbidity in GB - Bulletin 1 -OPCS - 1994
Dave Sheppard (ed.) - Learning The Lessons - The Zito Trust - July 1996
The Report of the Confidential Inquiry into Homicides and Suicides by Mentally Ill People 1992 Department of Health

INQUIRY REPORT 1 - JONATHAN NEWBY

TITLE: Report of the Inquiry into the circumstances leading to the death of Jonathan Newby (a volunteer worker) on 9th October 1993 in Oxford. Published July 1995. The report was commissioned by Oxfordshire Health Authority.

BACKGROUND: "On 9 October 1993 Jonathan Newby, a twenty-two year old graduate, working as a volunteer for the Oxford Cyrenians at Jacqui Porter House in Rectory Road, Oxford, was stabbed in the heart by John Rous, a resident in the house. Jonathan Newby died as a result of this injury" (p.3)

ROLE OF ALCOHOL / DRUG USE: John Rous had a long history of alcohol and drug misuse which was first diagnosed when he was 19 and pre-dates his diagnoses for mental illnesses. The chronology of John Rous's mental health contains 120 dated entries spanning his adult life. Twenty of these entries refer directly to alcohol or drug misuse. In 1965 he was diagnosed as a Drimanyl addict; in 1968 he was arrested in possession of amphetamines and later claimed to be both an amphetamine addict and methadone user; in 1973 he was again diagnosed as a drug addict and charged with possession of controlled drugs; in 1975 he continued using illegal drugs while on a depot medication; in 1980 he was said to have had a six month history of misusing prescribed drugs; in 1990 he was drinking on a daily basis and had problems with his increased alcohol intake; in 1991/2 he was again taking amphetamines. (pp12-22)

The text of the report describes in detail the events leading up to and immediately surrounding the stabbing. In September 1993 John Rous went on holiday with his day centre. Both prior to the holiday and during it, he is reported as having drunk heavily. (p.40) A month later on the day of the homicide, a witness described how he had drunk with John Rous. Four people, including John Rous, had shared four litres of cider and four cans of Tennants as well as sharing an eighth of an ounce of cannabis. Later in the day he drank another one and a half pints of lager. When John Rous returned to Jacqui Porter House he stabbed Jonathan Newby to death. (p.41)

In considering the influences upon John Rous's mental state which led to the homicide, the report identifies four factors:
schizophrenic illness
severe personality disorder
drugs and alcohol abuse
predisposing social circumstances
The report opines that "..the evidence is rather against an exacerbation of his schizophrenic illness. This illness would in part account for his long history of maladaptive behaviour and his consequent need to be living at Jacqui Porter House, but did not seem to have contributed to the immediate circumstances. There is ample evidence of long-term personality disorder and this was probably an important factor in his developing a habit of drug and alcohol misuse. A very high dose of alcohol consumed on 9 October and a considerable amount of cannabis could of itself account for an unpredictable, irritable, excitable and potentially violent mental state. When one takes into account the coming together of many deleterious social circumstances, especially those inside Jacqui Porter House, there is adequate evidence to explain his

abnormal mental state in the hour or two preceding the homicide and also how he could be impulsively violent to the extent of stabbing Jonathan Newby." (pp45-49)

RECOMMENDATIONS: The report concludes by asking agencies involved in residential care of people with mental health problems to consider:
"19.3.1 The programme of in-service training for employed staff and for volunteers should be intensified and be better directed to the needs of the severely mentally ill and the staff caring for them. To be more specific, without implying their relative importance or the amount of time that should be spent on each the following should be considered:
i. the signs and symptoms of major mental illness
ii. understanding and learning to talk with severely mentally ill people,
iii. substance abuse and its management: alcohol and drugs
et al." (p.151-2)

INQUIRY REPORT 2 - THE GREY REPORT

TITLE: Report of the Independent Inquiry Team into the Care and Treatment of Kenneth Grey to East London and The City Health Authority
Commissioned by East London and The City Health Authority.
November 1995

BACKGROUND: Kenneth Grey was born in 1970 (p.9), he "murdered his mother on New Year's Day 1995...By then he had been absent without leave for 30 days from a psychiatric ward of Hackney Hospital, where he had been discharged from being compulsorily detained under the Mental Health Act just some 4 hours before he went missing." (p.5) Kenneth Grey had no long-standing history of psychiatric illness and the entire period with which (the report has)...been concerned - from his first signs of mental abnormality to the date of the murder - spanned less than 3 months." (p.6)

ROLE OF ALCOHOL / DRUG USE: "From the age of 13 Kenneth started to use cannabis and then began to steal in order to buy drugs." (p.9) "He gradually began to experiment with other drugs... and had also been convicted for possessing cannabis on a number of occasions." (p.9) "In 1992...he was ..convicted of causing actual bodily harm and he said he was under the influence of drugs and alcohol at the time." (p.9)

Prior to sentencing for another act of violence in 1994, "he was the subject of extensive probation assessments....reports show that he had a serious drug problem and that he was maintaining that the reasons for committing thefts and burglaries were to finance his heroin addiction. It was acknowledged ... that he could not deal with his offending behaviour without first dealing with his drug problem....Kenneth was accepted by Phoenix House (a drug rehabilitation unit)...however he absconded from Phoenix House after only one day." (p.7)

It was while in prison after absconding from Phoenix House that he began to exhibit the bizarre behaviour which led to his transfer into psychiatric care. Questions are

raised in the report as to whether this behaviour was drug induced. It was thought likely that he had cannabis in prison, although there is no evidence of Class A drug use. One prison officer recognised that cannabis use was "endemic" in Pentonville but felt that Grey's behaviour was not drug induced. (p.17)
In the days between going absent without leave and the killing, Kenneth Grey admitted taking cannabis and heroin. (p.37) There is no evidence in the report as to whether he had taken drugs immediately prior to the killing. The report makes it clear that he was clearly "psychotic at the time of the murder." (p.10)

This leads to a debate in the report as to whether Kenneth Grey's behaviour was drug induced. The trial judge accepted prosecution arguments that the murder was the result of "a drug induced psychosis" (p.10) However, in a later section "The Diagnosis of Kenneth Grey's Mental Disorder" (pp.47-8) the report debates whether the underlying problem was drug or a mental disorder. The report is more sceptical about drugs being the key problem than the trial judge, however the report ultimately leaves the question open.

RECOMMENDATIONS: There are no recommendations which are specifically about alcohol or drug misuse. (pp.49-51) However one of the "Discussion" sections recognises that "as much of Kenneth Grey's offending seems to have been drug related and he was admitting heavy drug use at the time of his admission to Pentonville, this would have been an opportunity to evaluate the problem and set up a treatment programme whilst in prison." (p.20)

INQUIRY REPORT 3 - EB

TITLE: Report of the Independent Inquiry Team
Presented to Bromley Health Authority, South East London Probation Service, London Borough of Bromley - Social Services & Housing
Following A Homicide By A Service User in April 1996

BACKGROUND: EB was born in 1954. "On 23 April 1996, EB committed manslaughter. His victim was SB his estranged wife." In the preceding weeks EB had been resident in a probation hostel in Bromley and had been admitted and discharged from the a local psychiatric unit. However, the killing took place in Manchester, and the family had previously lived in the North East of England. (p.1) His mental health diagnoses were limited to depression and personality disorder.(e.g. p.13)

ROLE OF ALCOHOL / DRUG USE: The report records a long series of incidents related to alcohol misuse. In the period up to the early 1990's he is described as "drinking too much and concealing this from his doctors" (p.4) While in a probation hostel he was "drunk on several occasions" and "abusive to staff" (p.20 and p.22). While on an inpatient psychiatric unit in Beckenham, he reported that "he drank 10-14 cans of strong lager a day if he had the money." (p.24) In early April 1996 he returned to the probation hostel and asked for staff to take charge of his money "so that I could not go drinking." (p.38) In mid April, he left the hostel, in breach of his probation order. He went to Manchester to find his estranged wife. They are both reported as being drunk together on 18th April. (pp.41 and 49) On 24th April EB killed his wife, the trial judge remarked "It is perfectly clear that you treated her with considerable violence on this occasion in April this year when you were both in drink." (p.51)

RECOMMENDATIONS: The recommendations of this report make no specific reference to alcohol or drug misuse. (pp.57-9)

INQUIRY REPORT 4 - MICHAEL BUCHANAN

TITLE: The Report of the Independent Panel of Inquiry Examining the Case of Michael Buchanan
November 1994
Commissioned by NW London Mental Health NHS Trust

BACKGROUND: In October 1993 Michael Buchanan, a former patient of Shenley Hospital, was sentenced to life imprisonment for the manslaughter of 54 year old Frederick Graver. (p.2) The perpetrator was 29 at the time of the incident and in the previous ten years had been admitted to psychiatric wards on thirteen separate occasions. (p.2) He had a long history of being in care and is described in the report as lacking "consistent parenting". (pp4-5)
Michael Buchanan's exact diagnosis was difficult to determine. He is described at one point as having a "triple diagnosis" (p.18). These diagnoses were:
a psychopathic personality disorder
schizophrenia
"desire for taking illicit drugs" (p.16)
He also had a long criminal history ranging from shop-lifting and burglary to actual bodily harm. (p.6)

ROLE OF ALCOHOL / DRUG USE: This report is quite clear about the significance of drug misuse in Michael Buchanan's lifestyle. "(His) life has followed a similar pattern for a long period. A cycle developed which had been consistent for at least ten years:
-whilst in the community Michael Buchanan used illicit drugs and to feed his habit stole and committed other offences
-he was arrested often and went to prison or was placed on probation.
-his mental condition deteriorated and he required transfer to hospital.
-his mental state improved rapidly and he was discharged.
-in the community he would refuse medication and his mental state would deteriorate alongside his use of illicit drugs.
-he would re-enter hospital or re-offend to feed his drug habit and go to prison." (p.16)

Michael Buchanan himself admitted that "a number of his psychotic episodes were induced by crack / cocaine usage," although "there is strong evidence that he had schizophrenic symptoms in the absence of drug use." (p.17)

In the period prior to the actual killing Michael Buchanan had been discharged from Shenley Hospital. He began to commit "several serious and violent crimes in an attempt to obtain money for drugs." At the time of the actual offence Michael Buchanan had been smoking £100 worth of cocaine. (p.14) The report indicates that "at the time of the offence "Michael Buchanan was suffering from an abnormality of mind due to his severe mental illness of paranoid schizophrenia (and) was also likely to have been compounded by abusing crack cocaine and alcohol." (p.14) Indeed his whole history of mental illness "had been compounded by prolonged periods of illicit drug abuse including crack cocaine, cannabis and alcohol abuse." There had been past attempts to counsel him about this aspect, but all "had been totally unsuccessful." (p.14)

The report makes the point that "the closure of long stay hospitals...will affect the ability of locally provided units to care for patients with conditions similar to Michael Buchanan. A large institution located away from the deprived inner city areas, makes it more difficult for patients to obtain illicit drugs and alcohol." (p.19)

The report criticises the two psychiatric histories presented to the inquiry team because they failed to represent the pattern of substance misuse in the case. "Once the panel was aware of the extent of the drug abuse it was possible to understand more clearly Michael Buchanan's condition and history." (p.20)

RECOMMENDATIONS: This report identifies the central role of substance misuse in the events leading to the death of Frederick Graver. It has a separate section entitled "drug misuse" (p.20) and, as has been shown, acknowledges the failure of psychiatric services to fully report the substance misuse. However, the formal recommendations of the report do not have any specific guidance about alcohol and drug misuse (pp.23-25).

INQUIRY REPORT 5 - BRIAN DOHERTY

TITLE: The Brian Doherty Inquiry
Report of the Inquiry Team to the Western Health and Social Services Board
October 1995

BACKGROUND: Brian Doherty, aged 20, "discharged himself Contrary to Medical Advice from the Tyrone and Fermanagh Hospital on the same day that he abducted and killed Kieran Hughes. (p.1) He was sentenced to life imprisonment for manslaughter. Brian Doherty had contact with twenty different caring agencies over a ten year period prior to the killing. These included special schools, children's homes, a training school, various young offender institutions, the Probation Service and various hospitals." (p.1) The inquiry reports that the young man had no formal mental illness but rather a diagnosis of a severe personality disorder of the dissocial type and mild mental handicap." (p.2)

Brain Doherty also had a long history of offending and in the period immediately prior to the killing had been street homeless. (pp95-103)

ROLE OF ALCOHOL / DRUG USE: There is little evidence that alcohol or drug misuse was a significant problem for Brian Doherty either prior to the killing or in his earlier years. There is evidence of both glue-sniffing (p.23) and heavy drinking (pp.24 & 27) as a teenager, but nothing to mark this behaviour out from the general run of teenage experimentation.

It is, however, worth noting that Brian Doherty's father is described as having a serious drinking problem during Doherty's childhood. "When he was aged 9, the family broke up because of his father's drinking and aggressive behaviour." (p.46)

RECOMMENDATIONS: Not surprisingly, this report makes no specific recommendations about alcohol or drug misuse. (pp75-84)

INQUIRY REPORT 6 - ELLEN AND ALAN BOLLAND

TITLE: The Ellen and Alan Bolland Inquiry
Independent Panel of Inquiry into the circumstances surrounding the deaths of Ellen and Alan Bolland
Report to City of Westminster, the Kensington Chelsea and Westminster Health Authority and NW London Mental Health NHS Trust
March 1995

BACKGROUND: In March 1994 Alan Bolland strangled his 71 year old mother with whom he lived. In July that same year he was found hanged in his cell at Wandsworth prison. The inquiry was set up because over the nine years prior to the homicide, "Mr. Bolland was...an outpatient at the Paterson Wing (NW London Mental Health NHS Trust) ...for problems relating to depression and alcoholism." (p.2)

ROLE OF ALCOHOL / DRUG USE: There is little doubt from the report that his alcohol problem is a major factor in bringing Alan Bolland into contact with mental health services, if not the main factor. On first contact with Paterson Wing in July 1985, he was seen as being "Lonely, inadequate, alcoholic, paranoid, anxious, suffering from recurrent depressions and recurrently suicidal....He was never diagnosed as psychotic." (p.2)

In 1986 he underwent detoxification during which he suffered severe withdrawals. Later that year, after help from ACCEPT in West London, he managed to give up drinking until 1989. He then relapsed into a pattern of bout drinking. In that year he was convicted for assault and robbery while drunk. In October 1991 he was referred for counselling as a problem drinker. In October 1993 his mother brought him as an outpatient because he was drinking heavily every day and needed help. In the nine years of contact with Paterson Wing he was seen by some 20 junior doctors, whose letters to his GP all describe depression and alcohol problems. (p.11)

Alan Bolland was certainly having problems in the period leading up to the homicide, however the report does not make it clear whether alcohol was a factor in the period immediately prior to the killing. However, immediately after the killing and prior to his arrest Alan Bolland was certainly found to be drinking. (p.3)

RECOMMENDATIONS: Despite the fact that Alan Bolland clearly had a diagnosed alcohol problem and that this was one of the main causes of his engagement with mental health services, the report makes no recommendations about alcohol or drug misuse. (pp25-31)

INQUIRY REPORT 7 - THE FALLING SHADOW

TITLE: The Falling Shadow - One Patient's Mental Health Care 1978-1993
Louis Blom-Cooper et al.
Duckworth 1995
Report of the Commitee of Inquiry into the events leading up to and surrounding the fatal incident at the Edith Morgan Centre, Torbay, on 1st September 1993.

BACKGROUND: Andrew Robinson, a detained patient at the Edith Morgan Centre, stabbed and killed Georgina Robinson (an occupational therapist and no relation to her killer) at the Centre on 1st September 1993. Andrew Robinson, a man in his thirties, had a long history of schizophrenia and engagement with mental health services since he was a student in 1978.

ROLE OF ALCOHOL / DRUG USE: Generally alcohol and drug misuse does not feature as a part of the picture of Andrew Robinson presented by the report, nor did it appear to be part of the background to the actual homicide. However, it is worth noting that the first serious act perpetrated by Andrew Robinson, the firing of a shotgun as a student, was carried out after drinking 4-6 pints of cider, and against a background of heavy drinking during that period. The shooting is described as a rehearsal for an attempt to kill a person known to him. (pp.202 & 204)

The report carries a section on risk assessment with people with mental health problems. This recognises the significance of alcohol and drug misuse in risk assessment. (p.177)

RECOMMENDATIONS: Not surprisingly there are no significant recommendations related to alcohol and drug misuse.

INQUIRY REPORT 8 - RAYMOND SINCLAIR

TITLE: Report of the Inquiry into the Treatment and Care of Raymond Sinclair
A report commissioned by West Kent Health Authority and Kent County Council Social Services
June 1996

BACKGROUND: Raymond Sinclair stabbed his mother to death in November 1994. (p.47) He was a man with a long and complex history. He was taken into care in 1972 and remained in care until December 1979, having been subject to physical and sexual abuse by his father. He had several offences for theft and burglary in his teenage years, and in 1985 found guilty of making false statements to obtain supplementary benefit. (pp.10-14)

However, he had no engagement with mental health services until early 1994 when he appeared to have schizophrenic episodes which led to two admissions in the period prior to the killing later that year.

ROLE OF ALCOHOL / DRUG USE: Raymond Sinclair began drinking at the age of 16 and increased in his 20s so that by 1990 he was drinking up to nine cans of strong lager per day. He experimented with cannabis and occasionally took LSD and ecstasy. (p.12) The report is not specific on how this pattern developed in the period prior to 1994, except that in late 1993, Raymond Sinclair became a Christian and gave up drinking and smoking cannabis for a period. (p.13)

However, following his engagement with mental health services he is reported as drinking heavily on several occasions, e.g. in June 1994 he left the ward and went into Gravesend and came back drunk. (p.30) During his second admission in August 1994, he again left the ward and returned "smelling of alcohol." (p.39)

However, the most telling comments concern the actual day of the killing. According to the report at 5.00am on November 3rd 1994 Raymond Sinclair "awoke shaking from alcohol withdrawal", and at 8.00am went down to the shop and bought two cans of Holstein Pils, which he drank back at home. "Suddenly the voice of the "master" began to speak quite loud saying repetitively "kill her"." He then stabbed his mother to death. After the killing he went to the local shop to buy more lager and returned to the house. (p.47)

RECOMMENDATIONS: The report contains no specific recommendations about alcohol and drug misuse. (pp.75-77)

INQUIRY REPORT 9 - JASON MITCHELL

TITLE: The Case of Jason Mitchell
Report of the Independent Panel of Inquiry
1996 Gerald Duckworth and Co.
Commissioned by Suffolk Health Authority.

BACKGROUND: In December 1994, at the age of 24, Jason Mitchell killed a retired couple and his father in two separate incidents in his home village in Suffolk. He was sentenced to life imprisonment for manslaughter.

ROLE OF ALCOHOL / DRUG USE: There is no evidence that Jason Mitchell had been using alcohol or illicit drugs in the period immediately leading up to the killings. However, it is clear that he misused substances throughout his teenage and adult life (e.g. p.19). It is suggested that he had misused anything from LSD and cannabis (e.g. p.19), alcohol (e.g. p.75) and solvents (p.25). At times he was clearly a heavy drug user (pp. 75-6). One of his social workers expressed the belief that Jason Mitchell would steal to support his use of drugs (p.49). The report highlights that psychiatric services were constantly undecided whether he had schizophrenia or drug induced psychosis (e.g. p.15 & p.28). However, at least one consultant felt that Jason Mitchell was using substances and that these worsened his mental state (p.24). The report concludes in favour of a diagnosis of schizophrenia rather than drug-induced psychosis, but nonetheless recognises the important contribution of drug misuse to Jason Mitchell's clinical picture (p.40).

It is also worth noting that Jason Mitchell's father is described as developing a serious drinking problem during Jason Mitchell's childhood. (p.64)

RECOMMENDATIONS: This report reflects the role of alcohol and drug misuse more fully that almost any other comparable inquiry. There is a separate section which usefully reflects on the meaning, nature and relevance of the term drug-induced psychosis (pp.29-30) and on the use of drug testing in psychiatric care (pp.231-233). However, the formal recommendations of the report do not have any specific guidance about alcohol and drug misuse (pp.276-281).

INQUIRY REPORT 10 - GILBERT KOPERNIK-STECKEL

TITLE: Report of the Independent Inquiry Team into the Care and Treatment of Gilbert Kopernik-Steckel
Commissioned by Croydon Health Authority.
July 1997

BACKGROUND: Gilbert Kopernik-Steckel stabbed his mother to death and then committed suicide in Croydon on 14th January 1996. This report is unusual in that the perpetrator had had almost no previous contact with mental health service prior to the psychotic episode which led to the tragedy. At the time of the killing Gilbert

Kopernik-Steckel was a 33 year old architect working in Europe who had returned to his parental home while between jobs. He had seen a psychiatrist at the age of 18 following a shop-lifting offence, and he may have had a breakdown while in Paris, but he did not have a long history of engagement with mental health services.

ROLE OF ALCOHOL / DRUG USE: There is no evidence that Gilbert Kopernik-Steckel had either an alcohol or a drug problem. The report makes it clear that generally "his alcohol intake was modest" (p.11). Nor was there any evidence that at the time of the actual homicide and subsequent suicide alcohol or illegal drugs were influencing his state of mind. Thus, this report does seem to fit more closely the notion of psychiatric illness being the cause of the homicide. However, it is worth simply highlighting how alcohol still features in the overall scenario. Over the Christmas prior to the 14th January homicide, Gilbert Kopernik-Steckel had been observed to be drinking a little more than usual when at home. (p.11) Then on the two days prior to the incident, when the psychotic behaviour was really beginning to manifest itself, Gilbert was noted to have been drinking prior to a disturbance in which a kitchen door was pulled from its hinges. (p.12) Later that same day Gilbert Kopernik-Steckel had drunk three quarters of a bottle each of both vodka and gin.

It would be possible to ask whether the alcohol use worsened the developing psychotic state, but there is no evidence to support that in the text. However, it is reasonable to point out how increased alcohol use was, at the least, one of the indicators of the coming crisis.

RECOMMENDATIONS: The report, not surprisingly, makes no specific recommendations about alcohol or drug misuse.

INQUIRY REPORT 11 - CHRISTOPHER CLUNIS

TITLE: The Report of the Inquiry into the Care and Treatment of Christopher Clunis. Published February 1994. Commissioned by NE and SE Thames Regional Health Authorities

BACKGROUND: On 17th December 1992, Christopher Clunis stabbed Jonathan Zito to death on a platform of Finsbury Park tube station. The two men were complete strangers and the attack was completely unprovoked. Christopher Clunis was 29 at the time of the attack. Despite apparently having a good family and educational background, he had spent most of his adult years in or on the margins of the London homeless circuit, with a long history of engagement with mental health and criminal justice services. He had a diagnosis of schizophrenia and he appears to have attacked Jonathan Zito in a psychotic episode.

ROLE OF ALCOHOL / DRUG USE: The Christopher Clunis report is an interesting counterweight to the other reports in this study. In the second paragraph of the introduction the authors write:

"On frequent occasions Christopher Clunis told doctors, nurses and social workers that he had abused both hard and soft drugs from an early age; ...... he said he went to Eton College; he said he was born in Sudan. From the investigations we have been able to carry out none of these statements appears to have been true. Indeed there has never been any evidence that he abused drugs, save for his own assertions which assumed a truth of their own as the statement was repeated from one hospital to another." (p.7)

As this paragraph suggests Christopher Clunis often told caring agencies that he abused drugs (e.g. para 4.2.1 / 8.1.1 / 20.5.1), however when, for example, in 1987 he was tested for drug use after claiming a history of using substances, the test came back negative. This was a pattern repeated throughout Christopher Clunis's care. On a number of occasions drug induced psychosis was recorded as a possible diagnosis (e.g. p.17)

The point that the report makes is that there was possibly a degree of racial stereotyping in the assumption that Christopher Clunis would be using drugs. "Dr Fernando told us that in his view Christopher Clunis was probably suffering from a degree of depression, since he had never fully recovered from the death of his mother. In his view in treating black people, depression is often missed as a diagnosis but drug induced psychosis is too frequently ascribed." (p.12)

RECOMMENDATIONS: The formal recommendations do not include any comments specifically related to alcohol and drug misuse but the report concludes "we have not come across any prejudice or discrimination in relation to Christopher Clunis, save in a willingness to accept too readily that he had abused drugs.....we suggest that clinicians and others who care for black mentally ill people should not be too ready to ascribe odd behaviour to the abuse of drugs." (p.129)

INQUIRY REPORT 12 - PAUL SMITH

TITLE: Report of the Independent Panel of Inquiry into the Treatment and Care of Paul Smith
Commissioned by North West Anglia Health Authority
July 1997

BACKGROUND: Paul Smith battered his mother's boyfriend to death in Peterborough in November 1995. (p.9) He was 30 at the time of the incident and lived with his mother and her boyfriend, both of whom are described as violent, heavy drinkers. Paul Smith's history presents a classic picture of complex needs. He had a criminal record at the age of 13 and spent most of the period from age 16 to 26 in custody for acts of theft and violence. He only came into contact with psychiatric services in 1992 after his release from prison. However, descriptions of his behaviour in prison suggest that earlier signs of mental illness were simply not picked up. The three years between release from prison and the killing were ones of constant engagement with mental health services. After displaying symptoms of isolation/withdrawal and self-neglect he was detained firstly under section 2 and then under section 3. (pp.13-50)

ROLE OF ALCOHOL / DRUG USE: The report records a number of incidents when Paul Smith uses illegal drugs. These ranged from cannabis (p.24) to amphetamines (p.33). This is offered as a feature of his presentation rather than as a picture of a drug misuser. However, the more significant interaction with substance misuse is that both his mother and her boyfriend, the victim, are recorded as having serious alcohol problems (p.25 / 27) Their drinking made Paul Smith's domestic life very difficult, for example, one worker describes how the flat Paul Smith shared with his mother had been damaged by her boyfriend after both mother and boyfriend had been drinking heavily. (p.41) The flat was described by one worker as the "flat from hell" (p.35)

The actual killing occurred after Paul Smith had smoked a joint of cannabis and then became involved in an argument with his mother's boyfriend who had been drinking. (p.48)

RECOMMENDATIONS: There are no specific recommendations about alcohol or drug misuse.

INQUIRY REPORT 13 - THE WOODLEY TEAM REPORT

TITLE: Report of the Independent Review Panel to East London & The City health Authority and Newham Council, following a homicide in July 1994 by a person suffering with a severe mental illness.

BACKGROUND: Unlike the majority, this report chooses not to name the perpetrator of the homicide, choosing only to call him S.L. The report is, therefore, named after the chair of the panel Len Woodley QC. S.L. was a man in his mid 20's when he stabbed a fellow service user at a mental health day centre in Newham. He claimed to be under the delusion that he was killing one of the Kray's and thereby doing society a favour. Like the subjects of many reports, S.L. had a long history of complex needs, his mother had mental health problems and S.L. was taken into care as a child. As an adult he spent time in prison for robbery and had constant contact with mental health services who diagnosed him as suffering from schizophreniform psychosis.

ROLE OF ALCOHOL / DRUG USE: This report is quite clear that at the time of the homicide S.L. was not under the influence of either alcohol or illegal drugs (p.99). However, while in custody in 1991 S.L. was diagnosed as suffering from schizophreniform psychosis which was probably drug induced (p.26). Later in the years between his release from prison and the homicide, a general consultant is twice reported (pp.75 & 77) as having concerns that S.L.'s use of illicit drugs could interfere with his treatment plans. On the other hand, S.L. himself admitted using cannabis on and off since the age of 18, but that he had not used drugs in the months prior to the homicide.

RECOMMENDATIONS: There are no specific recommendations about drug or alcohol misuse.

INQUIRY REPORT 14 - MARTIN MURSELL

TITLE: The Report into the Treatment and Care of Martin Mursell, commissioned by Camden and Islington Health Authority, published March 1997.

BACKGROUND: In October 1994, Martin Mursell, a diagnosed schizophrenic, attempted to stab his mother to death and then killed his stepfather, Joseph Collins. The events occurred in the victims' flat in Islington, London. His mother survived the attack. Martin Mursell pleaded guilty to murder and attempted murder and is now detained in Rampton Hospital. At the time Martin Mursell was 28 years of age and had a long history of engagement with mental health and criminal justice services.

ROLE OF ALCOHOL / DRUG USE: This report is quite clear that "The mental state of Martin Mursell prior to his homicide was affected by mental illness, namely schizophrenia, and drug and alcohol misuse." (p.63) "There was a past history of drug misuse, including cannabis, amphetamines and heroin. The evidence of his drug misuse came from Martin who admitted to his mother that he took 'everything' in the way of drugs, which evidence was confirmed by his friends who told her that he did indeed misuse drugs. He also told Dr. Harvey that he had been misusing heroin from the age of 16. At the time of his admission to hospital in July 1994 marks believed to indicate injection sites were noted on his arms." (p.63) At another point the report writes that "A significant feature of Martin's life was his misuse of alcohol and drugs. When we visited him in Rampton Hospital, he told us that he was involved with drugs, mainly cannabis, since about the age of sixteen." (p.30) Yet the report does not explore whether this behaviour contributed to the chaotic lifestyle e.g. failure to pay his rent, poor state of his accommodation, which is described throughout the report.

The report recognises "Martin Mursell's case had variables which were associated with risk to others namely: previous violent behaviour and substance misuse." (p.66) Therefore, "..to discharge him from hospital and, eventually, release him from detention under section 3, was to take a risk. The risk was increased by the likelihood that Martin Mursell would eventually stop complying with medication and that he would resume substance misuse." (p.67)

RECOMMENDATIONS: The report makes no recommendations specifically related to alcohol or drug misuse, or the care provided to address Martin Mursell's substance misuse. However, it does recognise, in passing the dangers presented by alcohol and drug misuse and mental illness "..we were told in expert evidence from Professor Kevin Gournay that the co-existence of serious mental illness, in particular schizophrenia, and substance misuse significantly increases the risk of violent behaviour." (p.67)

INQUIRY REPORT 15 - THE VINER REPORT

TITLE: The report of the independent inquiry into the circumstances surrounding the deaths of Robert and Muriel Viner.
Published March 1996
Commissioned by Dorset Health Commission

BACKGROUND: On 19th April 1995 Robert Viner aged 42, killed his mother Muriel Viner aged seventy six. Robert Viner died some time later from a drugs overdose. (p.7) Robert Viner first received medical treatment for mental illness in 1971. Apart from two brief inpatient admissions to the Herrison Hospital in 1981 and 1982 he lived with, and was cared for by his mother, until their deaths in 1995. From 1976 onwards he had contact with mental health services in Dorset. The degree and nature of this contact varied over the years. The one consistent feature of his engagement with treatment is that he was on what is described as a "cornucopia of drugs" some prescribed some bought over the counter. (p.8)

ROLE OF ALCOHOL / DRUG USE: It is important to note that "no alcohol (was) found in the blood at post mortem and this argues against the homicide occurring in a state of alcohol induced intoxication." (p.11). Nonetheless alcohol featured throughout his life and in the period leading up to the homicide.

Early on the report states that "Robert Viner used alcohol as a tranquilliser in much the same way he used his prescribed and non-prescribed drugs. There was no real evidence to suggest that he became aggressive while drinking, despite taking fairly large amounts at intervals. The pattern of his drinking would be best described as one of psychological dependence....it would be fair to say that the situation was one of developing rather than established alcoholism." (p.11)

In a letter to a consultant psychiatrist, Robert Viner described his drinking thus "..bottle of whisky will usually stop almost all halluc. voices or else make you feel like you don't care anyway. However, it's too expensive (for me) and you can't get it on prescription or drive on it." (p.11)

However in the period leading up to the homicide Robert Viner's alcohol consumption appears to have been both heavy and a cause of concern for his mother. On the 13th March 1995, Muriel Viner was complaining about her son's drinking (p.12) On 16th April 1995 Robert Viner was described as having "drunk a certain amount over the weekend and spent much of the time in night attire." (p.13) On the day of the homicide itself, Robert Viner was visited at home by a community psychiatric nurse (CPN). The mother and son were seen to be arguing about Robert Viner's drinking at the weekend and "Muriel Viner asked (the CPN) into the kitchen to see two large dustbin liners filled with bottles all retrieved by her during the previous week." (p.14)

RECOMMENDATIONS: As in other reports there are no recommendations which relate directly to alcohol (p.101-105) However, Dorset Health Commission launched an internal inquiry which proposed to set up "dual diagnosis programmes for people with mental health problems who also misuse drugs/alcohol." This is commended by the inquiry team. (p.81)

INQUIRY REPORTS 16 & 17 - OTHER REPORTS CONSULTED

Report of the Inquiry into the Care of Anthony Smith
S. Derbyshire Health Authority & Derbyshire County Council
August 1996
There was no significant link with alcohol or drug misuse, although Anthony Smith had smoked cannabis and once taken magic mushrooms in his early life. (p.6)

Report of the Independent Inquiry Team into the Care and Treatment of SG
Ealing, Hammersmith & Hounslow Health Authority
April 1996
There was no evident link with alcohol or drug misuse.

CONCLUSION AND DISCUSSION

NB. It is of course impossible to make definitive conclusions about the role of alcohol and drug misuse from a simple reading of the text of the report. All the comments below must, of course, be regarded as tentative conclusions drawn on the basis of the texts rather than face to face contact with the people concerned.

The evidence of these reports speaks for itself. Even at a cursory reading, it is clear that drug and alcohol misuse features significantly in a number of the reports. However, in order to analyse the extent of substance misuse it is essential to have a some definitions of this vague term against which to measure the evidence presented. Substance misuse is not an absolute diagnosis. The debate about the definition of "drug misuse", "alcoholism" and other such terms has raged for decades and will probably continue to be exercised for years to come. For the purpose of this study the seventeen reports will be examined against following criteria:

- Is there any evidence of illicit drug use? *(Illicit Drug Use)*
- Is there any evidence of repeated or regular use of alcohol or illicit drugs which have led to social, physical or psychological problems? *(Problem Use)*
- Is there any evidence of dependency on, or addiction to, alcohol or illicit drugs? *(Dependent Use)*

JONATHAN NEWBY: John Rous was diagnosed as an amphetamine addict and had a history of heavy drinking. *(Dependent Use)*
THE GREY REPORT: Kenneth Grey had a history of drug use which demanded treatment in a drug rehabilitation unit. *(Problem / Dependent Use)*
EB: EB displayed repeated heavy drinking which led him to ask staff at his probation hostel to control his money so that he could not buy alcohol. *(Problem Use)*
MICHAEL BUCHANAN: Michael Buchanan's history of mental illness is described in the report as having "been compounded by prolonged periods of illicit drug abuse including crack cocaine, cannabis and alcohol abuse." (p.14) *(Problem Use)*
BRIAN DOHERTY: Brian Doherty had used solvents as a teenager, but there is no evidence of repeated, regular or dependent use. However, his father is described as a regular heavy drinker. *(Problem Use by Significant Other)*
ELLEN AND ALAN BOLLAND: In the report Alan Bolland is described as an "alcoholic" and received treatment from an alcohol agency. *(Dependent Use)*
THE FALLING SHADOW: Andrew Robinson fired a gun after drinking as a student, but there is no other evidence of illicit drug use or regular problematic or dependent drinking.
RAYMOND SINCLAIR: Raymond Sinclair had used illicit drugs and on the day he killed his mother he was suffering alcohol withdrawals. *(Dependent Use)*
JASON MITCHELL: Jason Mitchell is reported as using illegal drugs and there was debate as to whether he was suffering from drug-induced psychosis. One worker is reported as feeling that Jason Mitchell would steal to obtain drugs. *(Dependent Use)*
GILBERT KOPERNIK-STECKEL: There is no evidence of illicit drug use or dependent drinking. However, there were incidents of heavy drinking during the mental breakdown prior to the homicide.
CHRISTOPHER CLUNIS: There is no evidence that Clunis misused drugs, however, he was often apparently misdiagnosed as a drug misuser.

PAUL SMITH: Paul Smith used illicit drugs. More significantly, he experienced problems because of the repeated, problematic drinking of his mother and her boyfriend. *(Problem Use by Significant Other)*
THE WOODLEY TEAM REPORT: SL is described as having used illicit drugs in the past and there were questions about whether his mental illness was caused by drug misuse. *(Problem Use)*
MARTIN MURSELL: Martin Mursell is described as a substance misuser, regularly injecting heroin. *(Problem Use)*
THE VINER REPORT: Robert Viner is described as psychologically dependent on alcohol. *(Dependent Use)*
ANTHONY SMITH: Evidence of illicit drug use, but no evidence of problematic or dependent use. *(Illicit Drug Use)*
SG: No evidence of any use of alcohol or illicit drugs.

Thus on this basis, out of the seventeen reports consulted in this study thirteen present evidence of either problem drug or alcohol use or dependent use by the killer or a significant other. A further one report includes use of illicit drugs.

THE RELATIONSHIP BETWEEN ALCOHOL AND DRUG MISUSE AND THE HOMICIDE

The most significant question is whether there is a link between the alcohol or drug misuse and the homicide. Of course, the relationship is not a simple one. Looking at the evidence from these reports it is possible to suggest a number of ways in which substance misuse can be related to the homicides:

- The alcohol or drug misuse may be the real cause of the homicide e.g. Newby;
- The alcohol or drug misuse is immediate cause of a worsening in the mental state which precipitates or triggers the homicide e.g. Sinclair;
- The mental state which causes the homicide is worsened by a chronic history of alcohol or drug misuse e.g. Viner;
- The mental state of the perpetrator may have been disturbed by others alcohol or drug misuse e.g. Paul Smith.

Alongside these categories it is worth noting two further potential categories:

- The misuse of substances is an indicator of a worsening of mental condition which then leads to the homicide e.g. Kopernik-Steckel;
- The alcohol or drug misuse is misdiagnosed as being present when it is not, because of prejudice or lack of training e.g. Clunis.

Dividing the reports among these categories is necessarily a controversial exercise, being dependent on opinion rather than a scientific analysis of facts. However, alcohol or drug misuse appears to have significantly contributed to the homicide in nine out of the seventeen reports (53%). (Newby, Buchanan, Bolland, Sinclair, Mursell, Viner, EB, Grey, and P. Smith). Moreover, in some of these cases alcohol or drug misuse and not mental illness might be argued to be the main, if not the sole presenting problem. The Bolland inquiry and the EB inquiry are examples of this and others arguably fall in to that category, for example Newby, the Gray Report and the Michael Buchanan case.

No matter how the reports are analysed, the message remains the same - alcohol and drug misuse is a very significant factor in these homicide inquiries.

THE KEY CONCERN

As has already been said the importance of alcohol and drug misuse in these homicides is obvious from this evidence. But this is not the key issue. It is not really a surprise that alcohol and drug misuse features in the reports, although the extent of it was still a surprise.

The real concern is that there are so few recommendations related to alcohol or drug misuse. Only one report (Newby) of the seventeen listed had recommendations that related directly to substance misuse. A survey of the over six hundred conclusions and recommendations listed in "Learning the Lessons" reveals that only four relate to alcohol or drug misuse (Two in Newby and two others from the Armstrong report and the Dalson report which have not been surveyed in this study.) (pp.50-118)

It is a salutary exercise to compare the extent of alcohol or drug misuse in this report with the paucity of recommendations. If there is one area that needs addressing above all others it is this inattention.

WHY SHOULD WE BE CONCERNED?

It is not enough for a report like this simply to highlight the role of alcohol and drugs in homicides by people with mental health problems. It must also be shown that such a linkage actually matters, that it has some impact which needs to be addressed. There are probably many arguments for stressing the role of substance misuse, but there are three key points which need to be made:

- We are failing the victims of these killings. By emphasising the contribution of mental illness, without addressing the vital role of alcohol or drug misuse as a cause, a trigger or a contributory factor, then we are failing to put right the problems that led to many earlier deaths. Lessons have not been adequately learned and further deaths may occur as a result.
- Substance misuse services remain under-developed. If alcohol and drug services are to develop to meet these challenges, then the problems need to be highlighted so that commissioners and planners can build alcohol and drug misuse service development into the centre of their planning.
- To continue to emphasise that homicide inquiries are about mental illness, while failing to recognise the role of alcohol and drug misuse is not simply detrimental to substance misuse services. It also runs the risk of continuing to stereotype people with mental health problems as dangerous and violent, when in many cases it is either alcohol or drug misuse or the interaction of substance misuse with mental illness which is a key feature of the situation. As the Clunis Inquiry says "We feel that it is important to emphasise, as many witnesses have reminded us, that the vast majority of mentally ill patients are living safely in the community. Furthermore the vast majority of those who suffer from schizophrenia are also living safely in the community." (p.109) By underplaying the role of alcohol and drug misuse we are giving a misleading impression of the violence associated with schizophrenia and other mental illnesses.

WHY IS ALCOHOL AND DRUG MISUSE IGNORED?

NB. Before answering this question it is only right to acknowledge that while there are few specific recommendations related to substance misuse, such specialist services could benefit greatly from reading and considering the wide range of generally applicable recommendations such as those about communication and continuity of care.

There may be any number of reasons why alcohol and drug misuse is ignored in the recommendations of these inquiries. These may be as basic as ignorance of the importance of alcohol or drug misuse or a belief that substance misuse is a symptom of another problem and therefore not a central issue. However, there are three key reasons that this report needs to highlight:

Terms of Reference: At the most basic level the reason why inquiries do not comment on substance misuse is because they are not asked to. The terms of reference for inquiry teams will obviously dictate the content of the reports and the consequent recommendations. The terms of reference for the above mentioned reports do not generally include explicit reference to substance misuse. (An exception to this rule is the Paul Smith inquiry). If future inquiries are to recommend more fully on substance misuse, it would be helpful if this was set as a specific task in the terms of reference.

Approach of Alcohol and Drug Misuse Services: the key feature of many of the substance misuse problems presented in this study is a lack of motivation to change. Many of the clients, e.g. Grey, Buchanan or Bolland have had contact with alcohol or drug misuse services but have not shown any interest in change. Most of these substance misusers were in a chaotic state. Alcohol and drug misuse services often begin their engagement at the point when the client is prepared to change. This will not be helpful to the clients indicated in these reports. One could argue, therefore, that the reason for the absence of recommendations, is that the alcohol and drug misuse service options required by these clients simply do not exist. This report supports the further development of alcohol and drug misuse services, but this development must include services appropriate to the complex needs presented by the perpetrators of these homicides.

The Role of Alcohol in Society: With alcohol, in particular, society may have problems recognising its role in such tragedies as homicides simply because it is so central to our lives. The vast majority of people drink and are perhaps unwilling to recognise that such a familiar activity can be associated with violence and homicide.

RECOMMENDATIONS

It is not the role of this report to make detailed recommendations. The essential task has been to highlight the problem, it is for others now to determine whether this problem is important and then move forward on it. However, in order to initiate such activity five basic steps would seem appropriate:

1. The Department of Health should immediately initiate further urgent work to research and explore in greater depth the contribution of alcohol and drug misuse to investigated homicides by people with mental health problems.

2. The terms of reference for inquiries should have regard to the role played by alcohol and drug misuse. For example the Paul Smith Inquiry included in its terms of reference the requirement to explore "the appropriateness of the care plan ....in the context of ...his previous psychiatric history including drug and alcohol abuse.(p.7)" This should be standard in all inquiry reports.

3. When appropriate, inquiry reports should make recommendations specifically about the care of the drug and alcohol misuse component of the case.

4. Alcohol and drug misuse services should be routinely circulated with inquiry reports and should consider the lessons for them in those reports.

5. Mental health and alcohol and drug misuse services at both a national and a local level should collaborate to develop better service responses to the often chaotic, dually diagnosed clients presented in inquiry reports. However, this should not be at the expense of the wider group of people with alcohol and drug problems who are also faced with a shortage of appropriate services.